CHAMELEONS

by Sophie Lockwood

Content Adviser: Harold K. Voris, PhD, Curator and Head,
Amphibians and Reptiles, Department of Zoology,
The Field Museum, Chicago, Illinois

THE CHILD'S WORLD®, CHANHASSEN, MINNESOTA

CHAMELEONS

Published in the United States of America by The Child's World®
PO Box 326 • Chanhassen, MN 55317-0326 • 800-599-READ • www.childsworld.com

Acknowledgements:

The Child's World®: Mary Berendes, Publishing Director

Editorial Directions, Inc.: E. Russell Primm, Editorial Director; Pam Rosenberg, Editor; Judith Shiffer, Assistant Editor; Caroline Wood and Rory Mabin, Editorial Assistants; Susan Hindman, Copy Editor; Emily Dolbear and Sarah E. De Capua, Proofreaders; Elizabeth Nellums, Olivia Nellums, and Daisy Porter, Fact Checkers; Tim Griffin/IndexServ, Indexer; Cian Loughlin O'Day, Photo Researcher, Linda S. Koutris, Photo Editor

The Design Lab: Kathleen Petelinsek, Art Director, Cartographer; Julia Goozen, Page Production Artist

Photos:

Cover / 2-3: Martin Ruegner / ImageState / Alamy Images; frontispiece: Tim Flach / Stone / Getty Images.

Interior: Alamy Images: 5-bottom right and 30 (Dynamics Graphics Group / Creatas), 27 (Christoph Henning / Das Fotoarchiv / Black Star), 36 (Craig Ellenwood); Animals Animals / Earth Scenes: 19 (Paul Freed), 22 (Zigmund Leszczynski); Corbis: 5-top left and 8, 5-middle and 21 (David A. Northcott), 5-bottom left and 34 (Martin Harvey / Gallo Images), 10 (Anthony Bannister / Gallo Images), 15 (Joe McDonald), 29 (David A. Northcott); Digital Vision: 5-top right and 16; Getty Images: 4 (Photodisc); 12 (Heinrich van der Berg / Gallo Images / The Image Bank), 24 (Dr. Robert Munterfering / The Image Bank), 32 (Gail Shumway / Taxi).

Library of Congress Cataloging-in-Publication Data

Lockwood, Sophie.
  Chameleons / by Sophie Lockwood.
    p. cm. — (The world of reptiles)
  Includes bibliographical references (p.   ) and index.
  ISBN 1-59296-543-1 (library bound : alk. paper) 1. Chameleons—Juvenile literature.
I. Title.
  QL666.L23L63 2006
  597.95'6—dc22   2005024779

TABLE OF CONTENTS

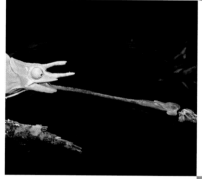

Chapter One

In a Madagascar Rain Forest

Darkness falls over Lokobe Reserve on Madagascar's Nosy Be Island. In the rain forest, night creatures emerge from their daily snooze. A playful lemur unwraps itself from its leafy bed. Shy black lemurs with their long bushy tails move from branch to branch in search of mangoes and tamarinds.

Fruit bats glide through the trees, hunting for ripe fruit. The fragrances of frangipani and wild orchids mingle in the air. A hungry Malagasy tree boa glides through the undergrowth. It is hunting for rats.

In the rain forest, the night is busy, bold, and dangerous. Maybe that is why panther chameleons remain nearly motionless throughout the darkness. Their skin color fades. In the moonlight, they look just like leaves on a tree. **Predators** pass by without ever noticing dinner on a branch.

Panther Chameleon Fast Facts
(Furcifer pardalis)
Adult length: 12 to 18 inches
   (30 to 46 centimeters)
Coloration: Aqua, turquoise, sky
   blue with yellow, white, and red
   markings
Range: Madagascar
Reproduction: 12 to 45 eggs per
   clutch; usually 2 to 3 clutches
   per year
Diet: Insects and other small prey

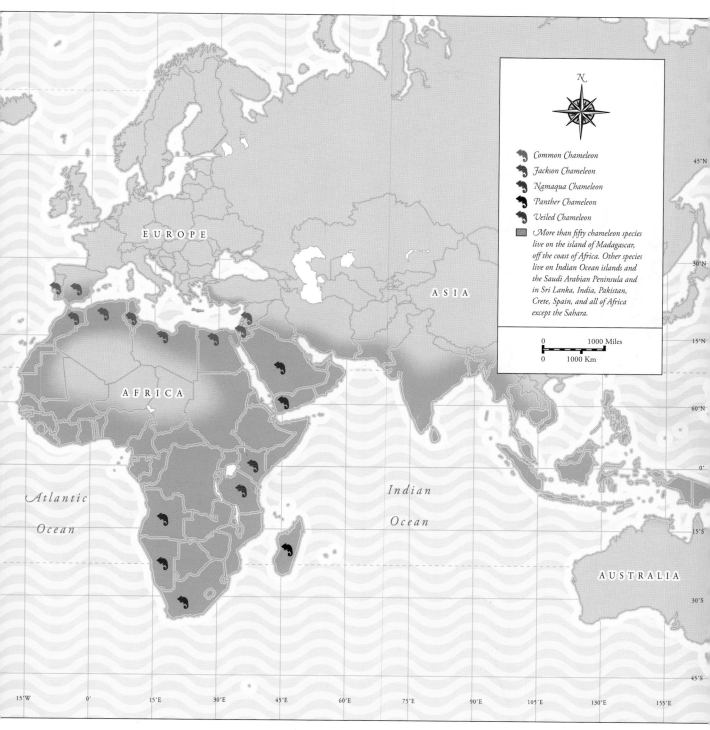

Common Chameleon
Jackson Chameleon
Namaqua Chameleon
Panther Chameleon
Veiled Chameleon

More than fifty chameleon species
live on the island of Madagascar,
off the coast of Africa. Other species
live on Indian Ocean islands and
the Saudi Arabian Peninsula and
in Sri Lanka, India, Pakistan,
Crete, Spain, and all of Africa
except the Sahara.

0   1000 Miles
0   1000 Km

EUROPE

ASIA

AFRICA

Atlantic
Ocean

Indian
Ocean

AUSTRALIA

15°W   0°   15°E   30°E   45°E   60°E   75°E   90°E   105°E   130°E   155°E

45°N
30°N
15°N
60°N
0°
15°S
30°S
45°S

This map shows the range of chameleon habitats.

As the sun rises, the panther chameleon prepares to feed. Panther chameleons are aggressive by nature. When calm, males are a pale lime green. When excited, they turn a rich turquoise with splotches of red, yellow, and orange.

A calm panther chameleons sits on a branch in Madagascar. If he becomes excited or angry, this chameleon will change color and display patches of red, orange, and yellow.

The male panther chameleon is quite comfortable among the narrow acacia branches. He uses his **prehensile** tail to steady himself. The acacia is in bloom, and its flowers attract insects. The panther chameleon only has to be patient. A meal will fly by in just a minute.

The male is rather large, about 18 inches long (46 cm). His tongue is almost 1.5 times as long as his body. That's nearly 27 inches (68.5 cm) of tongue. All chameleon tongues are sticky on the end and lightning quick. An adult male can shoot his tongue toward prey and have it back in his mouth in less than half a second.

The morning starts out with an array of flying insects and hairy spiders offering themselves as meals. The panther chameleon sways in the gentle breeze. His eyes focus on a dragonfly. Flick and swallow. A jewel beetle tastes the acacia flowers' nectar. Flick and swallow. A swallowtail butterfly ventures into the chameleon's range. Flick and swallow.

By midday, the panther chameleon has eaten a wide variety of insects, caterpillars, and even a small lizard and a tree frog. The tropical sun spreads its warmth over the Lokobe forest. An afternoon siesta suits the chameleon. He gives his trusty tongue a rest and settles down to bask in the sunshine.

Did You Know?
Madagascar women are forbidden to touch panther chameleons. Husbands cannot touch their wives for three days after handling a panther chameleon. And all traffic stops as a slow chameleon crosses the street. Running one over is believed to bring bad luck.

Chapter Two

Tongue Flicking, Shade Shifting

Chameleons are reptiles of the order Squamata. They are lizards that come in all sizes, from dwarf chameleons barely 1 inch (2.5 cm) long to giant chameleons that measure nearly 24 inches (61 cm) in length. There are about 160 species that are considered Old World, or true, chameleons. Veiled, Parson's, and common chameleons are Old World chameleon species.

There are thirty-nine species of dwarf chameleons, but that number can change. Eight new species of dwarf chameleons have been discovered since 1990. Dwarf chameleons live among dead leaves and low shrubs. Some are so small that a dozen can fit on an outstretched hand.

More than fifty chameleon species live on the island of Madagascar, off the coast of Africa. Other species live on Indian Ocean islands and the Saudi Arabian Peninsula and in Sri Lanka, India, Pakistan, Crete, Spain, and all

of Africa except the Sahara. Although most chameleons spend their lives in forests, there are species that thrive in desert regions, such as the Namaqua chameleon.

There are about thirty-nine species of dwarf chameleons. This one was photographed in South Africa.

CHAMELEON BODIES

All chameleon species have similar body shapes, head shapes, and teeth. Chameleon bodies have flat sides and a leaf-shaped body. The body shape helps the chameleon blend in with its environment. Some chameleon heads have crests, called casques. The casques are bumps on infant chameleons but may grow to 2 inches (5 cm) in height on adults. Chameleons have odd dental forma-

This Parson's chameleon, like all chameleons, has eyes that can work independently. Being able to see to the front and rear at the same time comes in handy when you are searching for food or trying to spot predators.

tions. The teeth are not arranged in sockets like human teeth. They are attached to the jaw edge, and all teeth are cone-shaped.

Chameleon feet are designed for tree life. Each foot has five toes. The two toes on the inside of the foot are fused together. The three toes on the outside of the foot are also fused together. This gives the feet a clawlike appearance. These feet are excellent for clinging to thin branches. In addition, many chameleons have prehensile tails that act as a fifth foot. This long tail wraps around a branch to steady the lizard. When not in use, the tail coils up.

Many lizards try to make themselves look bigger when facing enemies or predators. Chameleons take in extra air to puff themselves up. They are constantly on the alert, and their eyes scan the area for possible dangers. Chameleon eyes are fascinating. The eyes work separately: one can look in front while the other looks behind. When a chameleon spots a potential meal, both eyes turn on the target. Fast focus allows chameleons to catch their prey.

A chameleon's tongue is its greatest hunting weapon. Even a newborn chameleon can shoot its tongue toward prey and catch a meal. Chameleon tongues are one to one-and-a-half times the length of their bodies. These tongues work kind of like yo-yos with sticky tips.

SHADE SHIFTING

A male veiled chameleon adjusts itself on a branch. Veiled chameleons live in Yemen on the Saudi Arabian Peninsula. As another male enters the first male's territory, tempers flare. When that happens, colors flare as well.

Veiled chameleons are normally green with bands of gold, yellow, orange, and blue. When angry, their colors become brighter. For chameleons, color sends a message.

Chameleons do not change color to match their backgrounds. They change color because of changes in light, temperature, and mood. Chameleon skin contains cells that carry color or **pigment.** The pigment cells are in layers. Red and yellow **chromatophores** lie close to the skin. Blue and white chromatophores are beneath the red and yellow ones, deeper under the skin. The way in which the cells containing pigments expand and contract, and the way light is reflected off of them, contribute to the chameleon's ability to change color.

Like other reptiles, chameleons can't control their body temperatures.

Veiled Chameleon Fast Facts
(Chamaeleo calyptratus)
Adult length: Males: 17 to 24 inches (43 to 61 cm), Females: 10 to 14 inches (25 to 35.5 cm)
Coloration: Range of colors, including yellows, turquoise, purples, greens, and off-whites in a multicolored pattern
Range: Yemen and Saudi Arabia
Reproduction: 35 to 85 eggs per clutch; up to 3 clutches per year
Diet: Insects and plants (for the water)

Veiled chameleons live in a variety of different habitats in Yemen and Saudi Arabia, including dry plateaus, river valleys, and on mountains.

They bask in the sun to get warm or retire to the shade to cool down. A chameleon's skin tone helps it adjust to light and temperature. When the sun is bright, a chameleon might overheat. So its skin becomes pale to reflect the sunlight. A chameleon's skin is so sensitive that while it is fading to almost white on the side facing the sun, it can show normal colors on the side that is not in the sun.

In colder weather, a chameleon needs warmth. Dark colors absorb light and heat. A chameleon's skin reacts to gather heat, so it might appear dark green, brown, or turquoise. At night, when temperatures cool, chameleon skin pales to nearly white. In the shadows, the creature looks like moonlight on leaves.

Mood has a major affect on chameleon skin tone. Threat makes reds and yellows become more visible. An angry chameleon darkens with rage. When males want to attract females, they put on their brightest colors. They may go from brown to bright blue or from green to brilliant turquoise. Bands of yellow or red add to the effect. The females show their answer to a possible mate by changing color as well. One shade says yes, and another says no. A rejected suitor soon fades back to his normal color.

Chameleon skin reacts to light and heat, darkening to absorb the sun's heat when it is cold and turning lighter to reflect the sun's rays so the animals don't overheat when the temperature is high.

Chapter Three

Quiet Living

On a forested hillside in Kenya, Africa, a male Jackson's chameleon approaches a female. He's very excited, and his skin glows vibrant yellow, green, and blue. He hopes she will be interested in mating with him. If she turns a dark charcoal gray, she's telling him to go away. If her skin grows pale gray-green, she is accepting him as a mate.

After mating, the female becomes pregnant. Although most chameleons lay eggs on the ground in a nest the female digs in moist soil, Jackson's chameleons do not. Instead, the females carry their young in their bodies until birth. The birth takes place anywhere from five to ten months after mating. Our mother is relatively young and delivers ten babies. Older females may produce up to thirty-five young.

Each baby is born in a **sac.** They drop onto a branch and then slide to the ground. The sac rips off, and a live baby Jackson's chameleon settles in among the leaf mulch. The babies are tiny, about 1 inch (2.5 cm) long. It is a good thing that baby chameleons are fully prepared to

feed themselves. Once they are born, the mother departs and has nothing more to do with them.

Baby chameleons, regardless of species, cannot change color. They cannot do that until they are about six months old. That is when most chameleons are old enough to reproduce. They must be able to change color because color is an important part of mating.

Newborn chameleons eat the same foods as their parents. Generally, prey size roughly equals the size of

Jackson's Chameleon Fast Fact:
(Chamaeleo jacksonii)
Adult length: 7 to 12 inches
   (18 to 30 cm)
Coloration: Leaf greens and browns; males have brownish-purplish horns
Range: Kenya and Tanzania
Reproduction: 8 to 35 young per live birth
Diet: Insects and spiders
International status: Threatened

A baby Meller's chameleon hitches a ride on the tail of an adult.

the chameleon's head. Some very large adult chameleons, however, have been known to eat lizards that, head to tail, equal the chameleon's body size. Chameleons typically eat flying insects. They will also dine on snails and slugs, large spiders, earthworms, and caterpillars.

Most chameleons drink water as it drips from a leaf. They do not go to water holes or standing pools. Veiled chameleons and Namaqua chameleons live in dry regions where little standing water is available. They eat plants to get enough water for their bodies.

ADULT CHAMELEON LIFE

Adult chameleons spend their lives alone. The males and females come together only when it is time to mate. For most species, that happens once a year. The number of young produced depends on the species, age, and size of the female. A dwarf chameleon produces one or two eggs in a clutch. Jackson's chameleons can bear eight to thirty-five young. Veiled chameleons lay thirty-five to eighty-five eggs.

When a sea turtle lays its eggs, they all hatch within a few hours of each other. This is not true with chameleons. Eggs take from five to ten months to develop. Eggs in the same clutch may hatch at different times. The different births may be a couple of months apart.

The varying birth dates may give chameleon babies a better chance for survival. A mass hatching attracts too many predators.

Birds, snakes, and other chameleons prey on chameleons of all sizes. Larger adult chameleons are particularly dangerous because they are **cannibals.** They eat not only other chameleons but their own babies.

A three-horned chameleon catches a cricket.

Adult males defend their territories against all chameleons. As they grow more upset or angry, they change color. A panther chameleon hisses, gapes, and turns its body red.

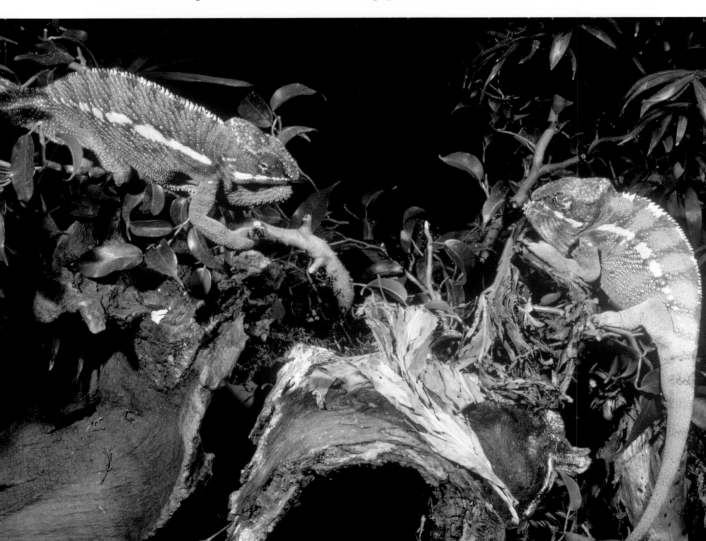

Two male panther chameleons face off. If one of them doesn't back down, they will fight until the weaker of the two loses.

He puffs himself up with air, and if his opponent refuses to yield, a fight to the death may ensue. Territory is a serious matter for adult male chameleons.

Some male chameleons have scaly, hornlike nubs on their snouts. Others have true horns. Jackson's, Johnston's, and Fuelleborni males have three horns jutting out from their faces. One is located above the nose, and the other two are close to the eyes. The horns are used as weapons. Males attack and gore their enemies, causing serious harm. To prevent injury, the weaker chameleon crouches close to the branch. He gives in to the stronger lizard and slinks away. The winner keeps his spot in his chosen tree or bush. The loser must find another home.

Most Old World chameleons rarely leave their tree homes. Dwarf chameleons generally live among the rubble on the forest or **savanna** floor. Their coloring blends into the splotchy greens and browns of rotting leaves.

In the wild, chameleons live from five to ten years, with males living longer than females. Normally, animals live longer in zoos because of regular food and medical care. This is not always true for chameleons. Capture and travel are exceedingly stressful for chameleons. In captivity, most chameleons rarely live for more than four years.

Chapter Four

Chameleon and the Creator

It is easy to trace the history of crocodiles and turtles. Their fossil remains tell us where, how, and when they lived. Fossils of long-dead chameleons are few. They can be found only in Africa and Europe, and these fossils tell very little about the natural history of chameleons.

That doesn't mean, however, that chameleons have had no impact on people who have seen them. Chameleons appear in many African folktales. The Bantu and the Zulu cast chameleons in the lead roles of many tales. In a creation story of the Yoruba people, Chameleon plays his role:

In the beginning of time, Earth was a marsh, an empty wetland. The gods lived in the heavens, but left the sky sometimes to play on the marsh. They slipped down to the marsh on long spider webs.

The Zulu people are the largest ethnic group in South Africa. They take great pride in their history and cultural heritage, which includes folktales that feature chameleons as main characters.

One day, Olorun, Owner of the Sky, called one of the other gods to him. "Take this snail shell down to the marsh. Use it to make firm ground."

The other god slid down to the marsh on a spider web. He placed the snail shell on the marsh. He had a pigeon and a hen, and put them on the ground, too. The birds scratched at the marsh and created solid earth. The other god returned, satisfied with his work.

Then, Olorun sent Chameleon to inspect the earth and see if it was true, solid earth. Carefully, Chameleon traveled to Earth on the spider web. He returned to the heavens and said to Olorun, "The earth is plenty wide, but not dry."

Chameleon returned to Earth a second time. This time, he found wide, dry land. Trees and shrubs grew. Animals were plentiful.

Olorun called the land Ifé. He made a house and called it Ilé. Today, the city of Ilé-Ifé is the sacred city of the Yoruba people.

OTHER CULTURES

A surprising number of people fear chameleons.

Did You Know?
Mark Twain wrote about chameleons in *Following the Equator* in 1897: "The chameleon in the hotel court. He is fat . . . but is businesslike and capable when a fly comes about."

This sculpture of a chameleon appears on a Yoruba palace in Benin.

In Benin, chameleons supposedly bring fire from the Sun. Some Africans believed the chameleon had the power to bring rain. In other African cultures, throwing a live chameleon into a fire is supposed to bring good luck.

Many Europeans saw that common chameleons could change color. They believed that a chameleon was not just a shade-shifter, but also a shape-shifter. They thought a chameleon's body could take on any shape. Their belief may have been based on the chameleon's ability to puff itself up with air.

In the days of early Christians, chameleons represented Satan who, like the chameleon, changed his looks to fool sinners. Chameleon eyes are uncomfortable to watch because they move separately from each other. In Rome during the first century, many people believed that chameleons could cure blindness.

Myths and legends with chameleon characters are popular. The chameleon has been paired with Anansi, the African spider folk hero. A Pygmy

Common Chameleon Fast Facts:
(*Chamaeleo chamaeleon*)
Adult length: 8 to 12 inches
   (20 to 30 cm)
Coloration: Leaf greens and browns
Range: Coastal North Africa
   extending into the Middle East,
   Spain, and Portugal
Reproduction: 20 to 30 eggs, laid on
   the ground
Diet: Insects and spiders

myth claims that Chameleon was responsible for a great flood. Chameleon heard a strange noise in a tree. Curious, he opened a hole in the trunk and water poured out. A flood covered all the land. Human beings appeared on Earth about the same time as the water.

Did You Know?
The Sufi Muslims have a proverb: "So, as the chameleon changes his skin, an unwise one changes the color of his being."

Chameleon's can rotate their eyes 180 degrees. This allows them to see in all directions while remaining perfectly still. Perhaps this ability is what led some ancient Romans to believe that chameleons could cure blindness.

Paintings and carvings of chameleons have been created for centuries. The true art of the chameleon, however, is its own colors, its own beauty. No manmade paint can match the brilliant turquoises, purples, chartreuse greens, and vivid yellows that paint the chameleon from within.

The bright colors of this panther chameleon communicate its mood to other chameleons.

Chapter Five

Humans and the Chameleon

A little more than thirty years ago, a pet shop owner in Hawaii ordered a few dozen Jackson's chameleons for his shop. The Hawaiian was delighted to receive so many chameleons, but he was concerned that they were in such poor health. They suffered from lack of water and from stress.

Thinking a bit of sunshine and fresh air would help the chameleons, the shop owner decided to put the them in his backyard. The chameleons rebounded quickly and ran off to parts unknown. It is the nature of chameleons to be hard to see in the wilderness.

The escaped Jackson's chameleons bred successfully. This caused a problem. Jackson's chameleons are an **alien** species in Hawaii. The environment is ideal for their growth, but they do not belong there.

Keep in mind that a Jackson's chameleon female can produce eight to thirty-five young per live birth. Within

six months, the females in that clutch will be old enough to bear young. Also, because the species is alien, Hawaii has no natural predators to stem their population growth. The lizards, birds, and snakes that normally prey on chameleons and their young do not live in Hawaii.

So after thirty years of population growth, the Jackson's chameleons have created a serious environmental problem. The offspring of those few dozen chameleons have spread from Oahu to Maui, Hawaii, and Kauai islands.

A Jackson's chameleon catches a meal in Hawaii.

The same species that is listed as threatened in Kenya has become an unwelcome addition to the islands of Hawaii.

SURVIVAL PROBLEMS

The greatest concern for chameleon survival is on the island nation of Madagascar. Most of the chameleon species found there live nowhere else on Earth. But Madagascar is a developing nation and has serious needs.

The island is home to more than 17 million people. These people need homes, food, and jobs. Building, farming, and timber cutting are important industries in Madagascar. To date, about 80 percent of Madagascar's native forests—chameleon habitats—have been destroyed. Land that the people there once held sacred has been taken over by chain saws and bulldozers. Clear-cutting the forest and burning the scrub destroys chameleon habitats.

More than two-thirds of Madagascar's people live in poverty. They have little food and few ways to earn income. The sale of exotic pets—chameleons of all species—puts money in their pockets and food on the table. It is impossible to convince a starving person that collecting and selling chameleons is wrong. Poachers can earn six months' income from one week of chameleon hunting. They are not concerned that 90 percent of chameleons shipped for the pet trade die during travel. They do not worry about the reduced life span of chameleons in captivity. They worry about feeding their children.

Among ground-living chameleon species, such as the Namaqua chameleon and the dwarf chameleon species, loss of habitat is also a problem. Human populations are expanding into the countryside. People take over chameleon habitats and turn them into front yards and parking lots.

Trees are cut down and the remaining scrub is burned to create new farmland in Madagascar.

Chameleons in South Africa, Angola, and Namibia face water **pollution.** Desert and ground-living chameleons drink from standing water. If the water is polluted with chemicals, chameleons take in poisons as they drink. In addition, these creatures often meet a new group of predators. They would naturally face snakes, birds, and other lizards in the wild. Now, in areas where humans have taken over chameleon habitats, pet cats, dogs, and birds stalk chameleons, too.

PROTECTING THE SPECIES

International **conservation** groups have serious concerns about the survival of chameleons. They worry because chameleon species now compete with other species for less habitat space. They recognize that chameleons are delicate animals that do not fare well with change.

The Convention on International Trade in Endangered Species lists twenty-five chameleon species as threatened. The group wants countries in which chameleons live to control the poaching and smuggling of them for the exotic pet trade. In addition, they have placed a total ban on trading in dwarf spiny chameleons because they are rare.

Namaqua Chameleon Fast Facts
(Chamaeleo namaquensis)
Adult length: Males: about 5 inches (13 cm), Females: 10 to 10.5 inches (25 to 27 cm)
Coloration: Grayish green to bright maroon
Range: Angola, Namibia, and South Africa
Reproduction: 6 to 30 eggs per clutch; up to 3 clutches per year
Diet: Locusts, crickets, beetles, lizards, small snakes, and scorpions

A boy shows off his pet Jackson's chameleon.

Conservation doesn't have to be a huge effort. It can be a small endeavor that saves a habitat or ensures survival of a chameleon species. In Durban, South Africa, plans were moving ahead on a construction site. Someone found that the site was also home to black-headed dwarf chameleons. Quickly, concerned citizens went into action. They looked for a new location where the chameleons could live. The new "chameleon park" would need a mix of reeds, grasses, shrubs, and tall trees. There had to be unpolluted water and plenty of leaf rubble on the ground.

For twelve nights, citizens collected the chameleons in the area. They are extremely small and difficult to find in the dark. They moved sixty-eight black-headed dwarf chameleons to the new location. This was a small event, but it may have saved the species.

What can you do? If you are interested in having a chameleon for a pet, be sure you buy one produced by a breeder, not taken from the wild. Learn all you can about taking care of a chameleon before you own one. Make sure that your chameleon has the space and environment it needs not just to survive but to thrive.

Glossary

alien (AY-lee-uhn) not native

cannibals (KAN-uh-buhlz) animals that eat the young of their own species

chromatophores (kroh-MAT-uh-forz) cells that carry color

clutch (KLUHCH) a group of eggs laid at one time

conservation (kon-sur-VAY-shuhn) the act of saving or preserving some aspect of wildlife

pigment (PIG-muhnt) a substance that creates a color or hue

pollution (puh-LOO-shuhn) the fouling of air, water, or land by waste, chemicals, or other contaminating agents

predators (PRED-uh-turz) animals that hunt and kill other animals for food

prehensile (pree-HEN-suhl) clinging or grasping

sac (SAK) a container or wrapping

savanna (suh-VAN-uh) a tropical grassland

For More Information

Watch It

Camouflage, Cuttlefish, and Chameleons Changing Color. VHS (Washington, D.C., National Geographic GeoKids, 1996).

Living Edens—Madagascar: A World Apart. VHS (Alexandria, Va., PBS, 2000).

Read It

Bartlett, Richard, and Patricia Bartlett. *Jackson's and Veiled Chameleons.* Hauppauge, N.Y.: Barron's Educational Series, 2001.

Deiters, Erika, and Jim Deiters. *Chameleons.* Austin, Tex.: Raintree Steck-Vaughn, 2002.

Schmidt, W. *Chameleons Care & Breeding.* Philadelphia: Chelsea House, 1999.

Look It Up

Visit our home page for lots of links about chameleons: *http://www.childsworld.com/links*

Note to Parents, Teachers, and Librarians: We routinely verify our Web links to make sure they are safe, active sites—so encourage your readers to check them out!

The Animal Kingdom
Where Do Chameleons Fit In?

Kingdom: Animal

Phylum: Chordata

Class: Reptilia

Order: Squamata

Family: Chamaeleonidae

Genus/Species: About 160 species

Index

About the Author

Sophie Lockwood is a former teacher and a longtime writer. She writes textbooks, newspaper articles, and magazine articles. Sophie enjoys writing about animals and their habits. The most interesting part of her research, Sophie says, is learning how scientists apply their knowledge to save endangered species. She lives with her husband in the foothills of the Blue Ridge Mountains.